A brave Chinese man faces down tanks during the 1989 student revolt in Peking.

Cornerstones of Freedom

The Story of
THE
COLD WAR

By Leila M. Foster

CHILDRENS PRESS ®
CHICAGO

Thousands of people gathered in Times Square in New York City on August 14, 1945, to celebrate Japan's surrender.

Copyright © 1990 by Childrens Press®, Inc.
All rights reserved. Printed in the United States
of America. Weekly Reader is a federally registered
trademark of Field Publications.

Library of Congress Cataloging-in-Publication Data

Foster, Leila Merrell.

  The story of the cold war / by Leila M. Foster.
    p.   cm. — (Cornerstones of freedom)
  Summary: Presents a history of the tense, often
combative, relations between western capitalist and
eastern socialist countries during the period following
World War II.
  ISBN 0-516-04750-7
  1. Cold War—Juvenile literature. 2. World
politics—1945—Juvenile literature. |1. Cold
War. 2. World politics.| I. Title. II. Series.
D843.F59 1990
909.82′4—dc20
                         90-2175
                          CIP
                          AC

Page 2: Hungarians carrying signs calling for
democracy demonstrate in Budapest in March 1989.

Page 3: Breaking down the Berlin Wall, the symbol of
the Cold War

Victory! On August 14, 1945, some 500,000 people flocked to New York City's Times Square to wait for the official announcement of the Japanese surrender and the end of World War II. When the news was flashed to the crowd around 7 P.M., the victory shouts filled the air. The killing had stopped. The Allies—the United States, Great Britain, the Soviet Union (or Russia), China, and the many liberated countries—celebrated. The Allies had beaten the Axis powers—Germany, Italy, and Japan—and the countries that had sided with them.

A jubilant sailor shows the surrender headline.

1939-1945 Hot War: The Prelude to Cold War

Six years of fighting in World War II (1939-1945) had left much of Europe and Asia in ruins, with millions of human casualties and devastated economies. Because the war had not been fought on the U.S. mainland, America was economically strong. Also, the United States had demonstrated its military superiority by dropping the atomic bomb on Japan.

When the Allied leaders met at Yalta in the Soviet Union in February 1945, no one expected the war in the Pacific to be over so quickly. President Franklin

Churchill, Roosevelt, and Stalin (left to right) met at Yalta.

D. Roosevelt of the United States, Prime Minister Winston Churchill of Great Britain, and Joseph Stalin, the ruler of the Soviet Union, met at Yalta to plan the next phase of the war. The United States and Great Britain wanted the Soviet Union to declare war against Japan and open up another war front in Asia. In order to get Russia's help, Roosevelt and Churchill agreed that after the war, the United States, Britain, France, and the Soviet Union would each occupy a part of Germany. The German capital, Berlin, was to be inside the Soviet zone. Soon after the Yalta conference, the Nazi war machine suddenly collapsed and the atomic bomb forced Japan to an unconditional surrender that ended the war.

The United States and Great Britain had a political tradition of democracy and an economic tradition of capitalism. The Soviet Union had a political tradition of dictatorship and an economic tradition of communism. These differences led to postwar tension.

With peace, the United States and Great Britain concentrated on getting their troops home and establishing a sound economy. The Soviet Union set about establishing Communist control of the Eastern European countries its army had occupied.

Churchill, speaking at Westminster College in Fulton, Missouri, used the phrase "Iron Curtain."

Winston Churchill speaking at Westminster College

> An Iron Curtain has descended across the Continent . . . Police governments are prevailing; and so far, except in Czechoslovakia, there is no true democracy . . . This is certainly not the liberated Europe we fought to build up.

President Harry Truman of the United States, angered by Soviet treaty violations and the spread of communism in the eastern Mediterranean, declared in 1947 that the United States would send money to help Greece and Turkey fight communism. This policy came to be known as the Truman Doctrine. Other European nations, still devastated

Harry S. Truman

7

Left: A parade in Athens, Greece, celebrated the arrival of the millionth ton of Marshall Plan goods. Right: Marshall Plan goods bound for Southeast Asia are loaded aboard ship.

by war, were suffering during the severe winters of 1947 and 1948. George C. Marshall, Truman's secretary of state, proposed the Marshall Plan, which would send aid to some 16 countries. Offers of help were declined by the Soviet Union and other Iron Curtain countries. However, both Russia and the United States supported the formation of the state of Israel in 1948.

Berlin, the German capital, like the country itself, had been divided into zones by the Allies. The Soviet zone became known as East Berlin. In June 1948, the Soviets blocked all roads through East Germany to West Berlin in an attempt to force the Allies out of Berlin. Instead, the Allies set up the Berlin airlift. For eleven months, 1,400 flights carried a total of 13,000 tons of food, fuel, clothing, and medicine into

West Berlin. The Soviet road blockade was lifted, and the United States had won world respect for its ability to meet the Soviet opposition.

The countries of Western Europe began a military alliance to fight the spread of communism—the North Atlantic Treaty Organization (NATO). Ten Western European nations were members, along with Canada and the United States. In 1949, Communists took over the government of China. Also in 1949, the Soviet Union exploded an atomic weapon. The United States and its allies had expected the Russians to develop the bomb in seven to ten years, but the Soviets had done it in less than five years. The policy now adopted was called containment—an acceptance of the Iron Curtain with an effort to limit Soviet power wherever possible.

German children cheer the arrival of an American plane during the airlift of supplies to Berlin.

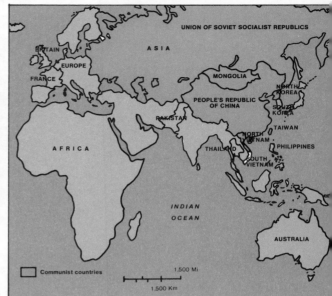

Left: U.S. Marines were part of the United Nations forces fighting in Korea.
Right: Map showing the countries governed by Communists

Meanwhile the Cold War heated up in Korea. South Korea had American-backed troops and North Korea had Russian-backed troops. In June 1950, the North Koreans invaded South Korea. The United States appealed to the United Nations (UN) to oppose the invasion. China and Russia backed the North Koreans. The United States and its allies backed South Korea. The UN voted to send troops to Korea. United States soldiers, along with troops from 16 other nations and medical units from 5 other countries, went to the defense of South Korea.

While the Korean War reached a stalemate, nations around the world began to recognize that traditional military forces were still important in the atomic age. European nations realized that it was important to build up the NATO forces. The U.S. Congress voted to send four American divisions to Europe as part of NATO.

1953-1960 Nikita Khrushchev and Eisenhower

Changes in the leadership of the major players in the Cold War came with the election of Dwight David Eisenhower as president of the United States and the death of Stalin in Russia. After a power struggle, Nikita Khrushchev became the Soviet ruler. Eisenhower worried about the domino effect—the fall of one nation causing the fall of the next nation like a row of dominoes. He challenged Russian aggression when and where he could.

President Eisenhower (left) with Nikita Khrushchev

Eisenhower agreed to an armistice in Korea largely along the original boundary between North and South. In Iran, the United States backed Shah Reza Pahlavi when Iran's premier Mohammad Mossadegh took over the Iranian oil fields from foreign ownership (primarily British). In Vietnam, Russia and China backed Communist leader Ho Chi Minh against the French, who were attempting to take back their colonial possessions in Indochina after the Japanese surrender. The French were defeated and Vietnam was split into two countries— the communist North and the capitalist South.

Ho Chi Minh

11

Hungarian rebels (left) capture a Russian tank in the 1956 uprising. Fidel Castro (right) speaks out against the United States shortly after gaining power in Cuba in 1959.

Behind the Iron Curtain, uprisings had been put down in East Berlin and in Poland. In 1956 in Budapest, Hungary, a demonstration turned into a national revolution. The new leaders even considered applying for membership in NATO. The Soviet leaders could not tolerate such a move. Eight days later, they sent in Soviet tanks to put down the uprising.

However, when Israel, France, and Britain moved in to take over Egyptian territory, Russia and the United States sided with Egypt.

Closer to the United States, Fidel Castro conquered the forces of Cuba's dictator, Fulgencio Batista, and allowed the Soviets to build a base just 90 miles from Florida. Since the Americans had a long-established naval unit in Cuba at Guantánamo, Cuba became the only country with both Soviet and American military bases.

In 1957, the Soviets successfully launched *Sputnik I*, the first artificial earth satellite. The achievement shocked the American people, who were used to U.S. superiority in all fields of technology. The U.S. rushed to catch up and the space race began.

In 1954 West Germany joined NATO. The Soviet Union and its surrounding countries formed the Warsaw Pact. Still there were attempts to avoid conflict. Eisenhower proposed an "open skies" agreement with Russia that would allow airplanes to monitor military buildups by either side. The United States also explored the possibility of putting a stop to nuclear testing as a first step in arms reduction.

In 1959, the Russians again demanded that the Western Allies get out of Berlin within six months. Eisenhower responded by inviting Khrushchev to visit the United States on the way to a summit meet-

Sputnik II, launched in November 1957, carried a dog named Laika into space.

A model of the first artificial earth satellite, *Sputnik I*, launched by Russia in October 1957.

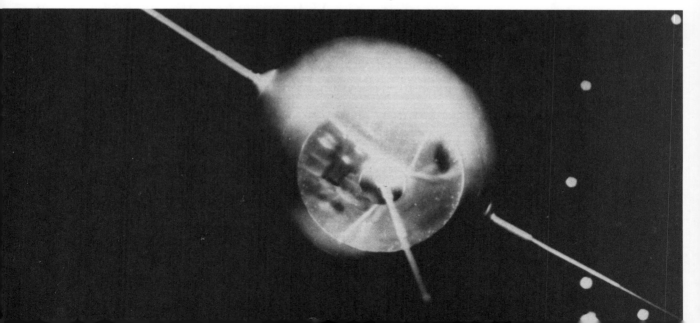

Left: Nikita Khrushchev denounces the United States while addressing the United Nations General Assembly in 1960. Right: Francis Gary Powers, the pilot of the U-2 spy plane shot down over Soviet territory

ing at which Berlin and other issues would be discussed. In the past, diplomacy was usually carried on behind the scenes by specialists in international relations. Now, and for the next nine months, world leaders conducted the foreign policies of their countries with full media coverage.

Plans for a four-power summit meeting that would include Britain and France were damaged when a U.S. spy plane, the U-2, was shot down inside the Soviet Union. The pilot was captured and held as a spy. Although the four leaders met in France, the atmosphere was strained. Khrushchev demanded an apology. Eisenhower said that the flights had been stopped, but he refused to apologize. Khrushchev then withdrew his invitation for Eisenhower to visit the Soviet Union and left the meeting.

1961-1969 "Let us never negotiate out of fear. But let us never fear to negotiate": John F. Kennedy

Left: A group of invaders taken prisoner at the Bay of Pigs. Right: President John F. Kennedy

John F. Kennedy was the youngest man ever elected president of the United States. He was also younger than most world leaders. At his inauguration, he proclaimed: "We shall pay any price, bear any burden, meet any hardship, support any friend, oppose any foe to assure the survival and success of liberty." Kennedy backed off from plans to intervene in Laos, near Vietnam, where a Communist rebellion was being backed by Russia and China. However, he went ahead with plans to support Cuban exiles in an invasion of Cuba. Unfortunately, the support did not include air cover, and the effort was defeated at the Bay of Pigs.

15

Left: Yuri Gagarin. Center: The last section of the Berlin Wall under construction. Right: John H. Glenn, Jr.

In 1961, the Soviets announced that they were closing access to West Berlin. Interference by the West, they said, would result in war. Kennedy responded that then there would be war. The United States began equipping troops. On August 13, East German Communists began building a wall between East Berlin and West Berlin to prevent East Germans from going into West Berlin.

In 1961, Russia's Yuri Gagarin made the first orbital flight around the earth. Almost a year later, John H. Glenn, Jr., made an orbital flight for the United States. Kennedy urged the U.S. space program to land a man on the moon by the end of the decade.

Meanwhile, the Soviet influence in Cuba grew. The U.S. Central Intelligence Agency (CIA) sent a U-2 spy plane over Cuba and discovered that the Russians were building launchers in Cuba—about ninety miles from Florida—for missiles that could be armed with nuclear warheads. Kennedy ordered U.S. ships to stop Russian ships from reaching Cuba with these weapons. After a week of world tension, the Russians agreed to remove the missiles.

Nationalism in Africa caused the breakup of African colonies into new countries—sometimes with Communist backing. South Vietnam asked for America's help in fighting the North's Viet Cong Communist forces. Kennedy responded by sending in almost 17,000 troops. Kennedy also sought to help

A U.S. Navy ship (top) sails close to a Soviet freighter carrying a cargo of missiles away from Cuba.

underdeveloped countries (sometimes called the Third World) through the Peace Corps. Many Americans volunteered for work in Latin America, Africa, and Asia.

In 1963, Kennedy urged a review of attitudes toward the Cold War. He wanted to relax tensions. America sold wheat to the Soviet Union during a time of crop shortages. In Geneva, Switzerland, the two countries agreed to stop nuclear tests everywhere except underground, where detection was too difficult to permit enforcement.

President Kennedy was buried at Arlington National Cemetery. Lyndon B. Johnson succeeded Kennedy as president.

On November 22, 1963, President Kennedy was assassinated. Vice President Lyndon B. Johnson assumed the office of president. Johnson concentrated first on domestic matters, building his "Great Society" with legislative victories.

Meanwhile, changes were taking place in the international sphere. Russia and China, which had been allies, were now hostile to each other. Khrushchev was dismissed by the Soviets in 1964.

In the United States, the Republican presidential candidate, Barry Goldwater, accused Johnson of being soft on communism—especially with regard to Vietnam. Johnson won the presidential election easily and stepped up U.S. support of South Vietnam. At the end of 1966, there were 450,000 Americans fighting in Vietnam. However, opposition to the war was strong—especially on college campuses. Other countries refused support because they saw the fighting as a civil war among the Vietnamese rather than a Soviet or Chinese expansion.

Marchers (left) protest the Vietnam War at UN headquarters in New York. U.S. troops (right) on patrol in Vietnam.

19

A Soviet tank moves into the main square of Prague to help put down the 1968 Czechoslovakian uprising.

In the Near East during this period, the 1967 Six-Day War resulted in Israel occupying territory formerly held by the Arab nations of Jordan and Egypt. In Czechoslovakia in 1968, a new leader, Anton Dubcek, attempted to abolish censorship and give the workers more say about the economy. Warsaw Pact nations sent tanks into Czechoslovakia, removed the new leaders, and installed Soviet control. United States negotiations with the Soviets over the Strategic Arms Limitation Treaty (SALT) were put off for a year.

1969-1980 Detente

Republican candidate Richard Nixon beat Democrat Hubert Humphrey in the 1968 presidential election. Nixon shifted the emphasis in U.S. policy from containment to *détente*—a French word meaning "relaxation of tensions." His adviser, Henry Kissinger, looked for ways of handing the Vietnam fighting back to the Vietnamese.

Probably Nixon's biggest achievement was the change in the relationship between China and the United States. China, under its leader Mao Zedong, had undergone a "Cultural Revolution"—a policy that forced many city dwellers onto farms and upset many traditional Chinese patterns. During that period, Chinese propaganda labeled the United

President Nixon talks with U.S. Secretary of State Henry Kissinger (left) and with Chinese Communist Party Chairman Mao Zedong.

Left: President Nixon and Chinese Premier Chou En-lai review troops of the Red Chinese Army in Peking. Right: A U.S. *Apollo* astronaut on the moon

States a "foreign devil." The United States had long been a supporter of the Nationalist government on the small island of Taiwan. However, with the Chinese Communist government firmly in control of a fourth of the people in the world, Nixon believed that it was in the best interests of the United States to change its relationship with China. Nixon went to China in 1972 and relations between the two countries grew warmer.

Other major events during this period were the 1969 U.S. landing on the moon, the 1972 SALT (Strategic Arms Limitation Treaty) limiting the growth of nuclear stockpiles, and the 1973 Yom Kippur War.

Vice President Gerald Ford took over the presidency when Nixon resigned. Ford met with Russian leader Leonid Brezhnev to begin the second phase of the SALT agreement about disarmament.

Ford was in office when the United States finally pulled its troops out of Vietnam. The North Vietnamese then took over South Vietnam. In Cambodia, a group called the Khmer Rouge, under the leadership of a general named Pol Pot, took control of the country with brutal force. Perhaps one-fifth of Cambodia's people were killed or died of hardships. The failure of U.S. policy to prevent the bloodbath that followed the withdrawal of U.S. troops from Southeast Asia weakened American prestige.

President Gerald Ford (left) and Soviet Premier Leonid Brezhnev met near Vladivostok, Soviet Union, in 1974. Bodies of Vietnamese float down the Mekong River (right) near Cambodia, in 1970.

23

Anwar el-Sadat, President Carter, and Menachem Begin (left to right) meet at Camp David

In 1976, Democrat Jimmy Carter won the election for the United States presidency. Carter made human rights a key issue in foreign policy — whether in Latin America or in the Soviet Union. He backed the Panama Canal Treaty, which gives the canal to Panama on the last day of this century. A SALT II agreement on arms control was signed by Carter and Brezhnev, but the treaty did not have enough support for ratification by the U.S. Senate.

Middle East problems loomed large. Carter attempted to negotiate a settlement between Egypt and Israel. Meeting with Egyptian President Anwar el-Sadat and Israeli Prime Minister Menachem Begin at Camp David in the United States, Carter helped the two reach an agreement, called the Camp David Accords, in 13 days of intensive negotiations.

24

The seizure of the American Embassy in Iran in 1979 and the taking hostage of Americans who worked there showed the hostility of the new Iranian leader, Ayatollah Ruhollah Khomeini, who had overthrown the shah. Soviet troops invaded Afghanistan to bolster the new pro-Soviet government that had seized power there in a military takeover. Carter saw the Soviet action as "the most serious threat since World War II." He increased the U.S. military budget, sent arms to Afghani freedom fighters, stopped grain shipments to Russia, and boycotted the 1980 Summer Olympic Games in Moscow. The period of détente, the relaxation of tensions, was over for a while.

Left: Blindfolded U.S. hostages in Iran. Center: Iranian students take over the U.S. Embassy in Tehran. Right: Soviet tanks rumble into the Afghan capital of Kabul.

President Reagan visits with British Prime Minister Margaret Thatcher.

1980-1988 "We must be strong enough to create peace where it does not exist, and be strong enough to protect it where it does": Ronald Reagan

When Republican Ronald Reagan won the election in 1980 for the presidency of the United States, he viewed the Soviets as determined to extend the Communist system through world revolution.

In Great Britain in 1979, Conservative party leader Margaret Thatcher became prime minister — the first woman to hold that office. She also took a tough line in foreign policy. Thatcher and Reagan worked well together and formed a close alliance of the two nations.

Reagan used military force against a leftist

government in Grenada. He sent a peacekeeping force to Lebanon. He bombed Libya in response to international terrorists based in that country. He supported anti-Communist governments in El Salvador and backed the Nicaraguan *contras*, who fought against the pro-Soviet leaders in their country. Arms were also supplied to the rebels fighting in Afghanistan.

In the Soviet Union, Brezhnev died in 1982. He was followed in office by 70-year-old Yuri Andropov, who died after 15 months. The next leader, Konstantin Chernenko, aged 72, died after about a year. When Mikhail Gorbachev took over as general secretary of the Soviet Communist party in 1985, he was only 54. Gorbachev was popular on for-

Left: U.S. invasion forces in Grenada. Right: Nicaraguan *contras* load a boat with supplies before going on patrol.

eign tours, but he had problems with the Soviet economy and with communist countries such as Poland. The leader of Poland's Solidarity labor union, Lech Walesa, was challenging Russia's policies.

Meetings between Reagan and Gorbachev in 1985 in Geneva, in 1986 in Iceland, in 1987 in Washington, and in 1988 in Moscow resulted in treaties eliminating short- and medium-range missiles from Europe. Reagan continued to press for the human rights of Soviet citizens. He negotiated from military strength, which included plans for the Strategic Defense Initiative (SDI), also called Star Wars.

Left: Lech Walesa, leader of Poland's Solidarity trade union, addresses a crowd of workers. Right: President Reagan and Soviet Premier Mikhail Gorbachev exchange copies of an arms-control treaty.

Left: A young man waves a flag with the Communist emblem cut out during demonstrations against the government in Romania. Right: Young people celebrate on the Berlin Wall as the Communist government of East Germany collapses.

1989-1990 Hot Peace

The year 1989 turned out to be a remarkable one. Soviet troops retreated from Afghanistan. In Poland, Solidarity beat the Communist government in elections. The people opposed and took over the Communist governments in Hungary, East Germany, Czechoslovakia, and Romania. The Berlin Wall came down and plans for reunification of West and East Germany began. Students in China revolted but their movement was crushed by the army.

In Latin America, attempts were made to unseat

Manuel Noriega

Manuel Noriega, the dictator in Panama. Eventually, American troops were sent in, Noriega was captured, and leaders pledged to democracy took power. In Nicaragua, the people voted out the pro-Soviet government. New peace plans were proposed in the Middle East. South Africa proposed changes in the apartheid laws that discriminate against blacks and other racial groups.

The Soviet Union experienced economic hardship. Government-run businesses and industries were not working. Gorbechev set a goal of *perestroika*—the restructuring of the Soviet system—to provide *glasnost*—greater freedom. He was voted new powers as the leader of the government, while the Communist party gave up its exclusive rights to control the country. Some of the republics that make up the Soviet Union voted to become independent from the Soviet Union.

In May of 1990 President George Bush met with Gorbachev to discuss economic and political issues.

The world may be leaving more than 40 years of Cold War for a Hot Peace of great change. Problems still remain. Will the people of the Soviet Union accept the hardships they will face as their country changes? Will a unified Germany and an economically powerful Japan be too much of a threat to countries with bitter memories of World War II?

Will nations trying to change over to free-market economies be able to succeed? Will new dictatorships spring up to replace old communist governments? Will leaders who favor free enterprise and democracy stay in power? Can the world deal effectively with the problems of cheaply manufactured chemicals for warfare? Can we establish international drug control?

When icebergs break off from a glacier, navigation becomes more hazardous on the seas. So the seas of diplomacy may be more hazardous today as political blocs and nations break off old alliances and face the many challenges that have surfaced in 1989 and 1990.

President Bush and Mikhail Gorbachev shake hands at a White House meeting in May 1990.

31

A young German chips away at the Berlin Wall in the shadow of the Brandenburg Gate, symbol of the old united Germany.

INDEX

About the Author:

   Leila Merrell Foster is a lawyer, United Methodist minister, and clinical psychologist with degrees from Northwestern University and Garrett Evangelical Theological Seminary. She is the author of books and articles on a variety of subjects.